D1516007

This book was made possible
by the generous support of the Estate of EMK

# RADIOGRAPHY

POEMS BY
BRUCE BOND

BOA Editions, Ltd. ❧ Rochester, NY ❧ 1997

LC #: 97–72083
ISBN: 1–880238–51–9 paper

First Edition
97 98 99 00  7 6 5 4 3 2 1

Publications by BOA Editions, Ltd.—
a not-for-profit corporation under section 501 (c) (3)
of the United States Internal Revenue Code—
are made possible with the assistance of grants from
the Literature Program of the New York State Council on the Arts,
and the Literature Program of the National Endowment for the Arts,
the Lannan Foundation, the Sonia Raiziss Giop Charitable Foundation,
the Eric Mathieu King Fund of The Academy of American Poets,
as well as from the Rochester Area Community Foundation Community Arts
Fund administered by the Arts & Cultural Council for Greater Rochester,
the County of Monroe, NY,
and from many individual supporters.

Cover Design: Daphne Poulin-Stofer
Cover Art: "The Repentant Magdalene" by George de La Tour,
c. 1640, oil on canvas, National Gallery of Art, Washington
Author Photo: Bill Youngblood
Typesetting: Richard Foerster
Printed in the United States by McNaughton & Gunn
BOA Logo: Mirko

BOA Editions, Ltd.
Alexandra Northrop, Chair
A. Poulin, Jr., President & Founder (1976–1996)
260 East Avenue
Rochester, NY 14604

# CONTENTS

## I.

## II.

## III.

# IV.

♣

# RADIOGRAPHY

*You are born; you live; everyone does it, with an animal force of blindness. Woe unto you if you want the human gaze, if you want to know what's happening to you.*

—Hélène Cixous

# I.

# NATIVE TONGUE

To glimpse it lounging in the red clay,
blind as a worm and skinless, shot through
with bluish veins and a craze of fibers,
any wonder we tend to conceal it?
To feel the full length of it, the appalling

ligament braided in our throat and bound there,
so tempting just to bury it in words,
and why not? The way it beats itself
senseless, flitting about like a bird
in a closet, what life is that? and whose?

Still you must confess: it's less disquieting
than going tongueless, and life enough
to rise up in spite of us, peering
over the rims of teeth, anxious to please.
God knows what possesses it to try,

as if it could tunnel back to some world
it lost, some day when it was little but
hunger and nonsense, and the body tangled
in its root felt less intimate or strange.
Given time it became the odd sister

of our two hands, a kind of bridge between
the body and the air that walks it.
And we swore—it was all we could do—nothing
would tear this wick from the lamp of the skull,
this rude animal from a swarm of angels.

♣

# NAKED EYE

The least touchable of all things,
it wears our dwindled world

like a prayer on a pin, shies
away from the slightest dust,

the stray lash, a blur of flies.
Our own hands are never pure enough.

We balance lenses on our fingers
poised near the shuddering surface.

Still it would be everywhere,
there in its pool the black anemone

blooming: you understand:
how it stares hours in the dim

TV light, reluctant to close,
turns red with so much going forward.

Even in our sleep, shadows
startle from the path it blazes.

It's the eye's way of waking
before the body, of burning

the world's remains to see by.
What could be more estranging,

more intricately shattered
than the prism in it, this iris

bristling with tiny filaments?
We love how the broken colors

streak out of the dark, expelled.
Small wonder, our passion for windows,

if only for their charity,
for the way we forget they're there.

Even stained glass takes us through
its body, the old wounds reddening

with promise. We come to expect them.
Nights when a wall and its window

darken to their merest difference,
our pupils brighten into beads of oil.

This too is how our needs precede us,
like a silent language of nerves,

the straight beam of a singular life

bearing down. If you look close,
you can see your own gaze floating

on its lens. Or thrown under, say,
the way one mirror rushes into another.

# POMEGRANATE

*for L.K.*

You could be turning it in your fingers like a planet.
A knife would do, if you're good with knives,
bracing the hard fruit in your slender hand;
a knife and a narrow gaze to guide it.
You brush a fly from your lip, quiet your breath.

Then there's the sound a vow makes when it shatters,
and the shallow fissure splits and reddens.
And all for this: a stain running out of a maze,
its honeycomb filled with dead sweet bees.
Your hunger is a straight line, pinned and singing.

It's only now you realize what you craved,
how shyly you ripened into a panic.
As for the shiny rivulets of juice
you chose your eyes to drink, who's to say
it was their freshness that drew you? All those times

you slipped your tongue into the bright tomb
the way a moth enters a jar of lamplight.
You know the place, how its mouth meets yours.
And now wherever you leave, it's winter.
You go to the window and wait, stare, turn away,

and the long night trails you like a gown.
Even in March as you return to all
your name's sake, what flowers you see are the tips
of buried fingers, each red flame bursting
through the earthly crust, calling you down.

❧

# CARAVAGGIO: THE SUPPER AT EMMAUS

Some days our very sustenance is desire.
A coal of bread warms its bright plate.
Pears blush, radiant and cold.
Even the dead appear in light of their need.
They rise in bowls, flare up on the lips

of glasses. They want us to remember,
clear to the last glimmering fragment.
Knives clink. A goat bleats at the door.
The faintest sound is bliss.
And so the joy of our disbelief:

this painting of Rome remembering Emmaus.
The studio smells of charred grouse and wine,
the drying canvas, a palette dish smeared
in amber and black. It is an unlikely story:
how the man the others took for dead is

crossing the beam of their recognition.
It was something in his hand, the way it moved,
making its x in air over the cooked bird.
Shadows flit against the walls like pigeons.
How trying it must be, playing the revived

in the swelter and dust of southern Rome,
holding your dead arms up for hours, amazed,
your faithless legs eroding into sleep,
while the man at the vanishing point of your story
draws back the heavy cloth of heaven,

his red robe made fierce in the light,
his eyes too calm with the poverty
of knowing. If I slide now toward his past,
it is only to look forward at these
glimmering fragments. They wander in rooms,

abandoned to a life, circle the place
where the light is deepest. There is no end
to the stream of people who pause here,
look, complete the motion of his hand,
and walk away. In my clearest memory,

he is a still feast. Though I imagine
he too is hungry, a man whose reach is
fleshed into our gaze, there, wearing
the brief afflatus of our wonder,
and a crown of shade, as all things here.

♣

# CARDINAL

Early when the cold light mirrors off
our picture window, I hear him flying
into the glass again, the tick and scoff
of his claws as he takes on the something
there, the impostor. It's in his blood,
the way he rushes into himself like one
flame into another, stunned and shuddering.
I get so little sleep, and wonder
in that half-sense of being foolish
if it's true, how those flown through the mirror
of a loss come back to pound and flash.
They want in, back to the fire
of April consuming us, even
as we half sleep, flying out to meet them.

♣

# BOOK OF THE LIVING

The whites of my eyes are never clear,
not white exactly, more the shade
of aged paper so much light

to absorb, and dark, so much
bearing up under the language
of unspoken things—bad grief,

bad rage, my inconsiderate ways.
What I know as myself shuffles
the pages in its dishevelled file,

sleepless for some certainty
I cannot love. I read once
the blood in our veins is blue:

I want to believe that: how we live
in a deep tangle of ink, blue
until it breaks to the surface,

brightening. Irrepressible,
this fascination and quiet
dread for how a body opens.

Nights I pour over tireless drafts;
the red ledger under its lamp,
a crimped page of one love's body,

the whole eroding chronicle
of a man with a woman's face
tattooed on his chest, her head rimmed

in a scar of flowers, deathless.
In time her name turns bitter,
the whirled cursive surviving

its occasion, breeding more names.
A rose-tipped needle plants its script,
and the vines spill over his fingers.

They grow unscrupulous as maps,
greedy for the uncharted regions
of his throat, his chin. Over his lips.

They cover his eyelids in shatter
patterns and small blossoms: so
when he sleeps, he is wholly illusion.

My waking interrupts his story,
and there are places on my wife's skin
where I imagine an intricate sadness.

Her hands gather beneath her chest.
They cannot know what leaves or enters
through these places. She turns away, groans.

This too is how a body opens,
like an obscure and beautiful book.
I get up so as not to wake her

and walk lightly through our dark house,
the empty narrative of rooms,
a leaky radio talking in its sleep.

I always wanted the future to arrive
without ceasing to be the future.
What cure? save the still music

of another life: the nimbus
of a tuning fork that dies when touched.
We may gape a little at hymns

like shirts on a line, bemused,
swelling into the hollow vowels.
We may magnify our wants

in the cavernous vaults
of basilicas and throats.
On summer lawns, the young are slitting

their wrists for an absence of words.
To stand on the edge of a high
dive as a child and feel the future

hurled upward in mockery and triumph,
to waver there a while in no wind,
it's part of what makes the skin skin.

My father knows this. He sleeps
to imagine his sleeping body
opening under the surgeon's hands.

What it wouldn't give to survive
itself, to outlive the book,
its story consumed in the vital fever.

As his ribs make their gradual way
to the surface, his lungs brandish
their shield, afraid for his diminishing

freedoms: how he sits up in bed,
sparks a match with his thumbnail,
coughs into his morning cigarette.

How small he's grown; like a name
for the loss of that particular name,
read only by a single god.

If he looks up, it's over the sense
of unfinished work, his torso bent
like a clerk's under the one light.

When he doubles over, turning away
the flushed coal of his face,
the pen quickens over his heart

monitor. Its dissolving streak
splits the dark glass—all night it cuts—
and the bright slash closes like a wound.

♣

# HOST

My father's body is the narrow grave
where they buried another man's heart alive.
Sometimes when he walks, he shakes a little,
unsure of the vital debt he carries.
When he pauses on the stairs, panting,

it is another man's flush he feels,
another man's sudden breath and shiver.
When he reaches for the words,
they come down just so far and wait.
The room he's in is another man's silence.

Some nights it burns at the center, this quiet
passing through him like a torch.
I worry naturally though for him
death is less than solitary,
less the dire property it was.

Every common kindness now, each warm meal
and paper cup of pills, is the unbroken
emblem of itself. At the root
of his pale throat is a gift,
a dark-red fruit too deep to harvest.

When he closes his eyes, he sees
the opening jaw of his ribs,
ravenous and steaming, taking in
the live bread. When the flesh goes vivid,
startled with blood,

it becomes the mourning tongue in his chest.
He could listen for hours lulled
by the faint sound on his pillow,
so distant there in the wet dark, his ear
pressed to the sternum of the world.

**II.**

# POSTCARD OF ATOMIC BOMB TEST, YUCCA FLAT, 1953

Say there is an explosion so great it shakes off
its boom and tremor and the voices
of those who watch huddled in their thin coats,
shivering, thrilled, stiff as matches,
and where they stand just shy of the cattle wire
they feel a broken aftermath of air
breezing through them in a fine snow.

Then just as suddenly you are there
and you've always been there,
a printed figure on a postcard snapshot,
made ancient, beautiful in your smallness
like a waterboy under a Japanese mountain,
your legs shimmering in a photo blur,
under your feet a plate of floodlight.

You feel yourself rising like a morsel,
a slice, something offered to a guest,
and all around you the desert cicadas
freeze up in their armor, and every desire
is the gray night coming into focus.
A kind of blessing, you tell yourself,
how nothing so still could be true

or complete, as if the world's crust
were the ashen face in an open casket—
illusion really, a shadowplay,
and that's why you stare, gazing out
through smoked lenses at the dry
cloud blooming in the distance,
because to stare this long and hard

makes the night sky sheer, translucent,
the sky and the tiny pins of ink
that hold you to it. It is 1953.
You are whispering something under your breath.
Every day is a day in June
at twilight. This is only a test,
you tell yourself, only a test.

## NORTH: 1991

In the euphoria that followed
the American air strike
when the New York Exchange soared

over the smoldering cities
and hovered there, a frail spire
aimed at heaven, I was driving

North, like so many who work
in town and live in the canyon.
It was the one road along the icy river

through the narrow tunnel
of my light, the radio cupping
a last match of news in its palm:

I live so close to nowhere.
I've driven this route ten winters,
and never was it so difficult

under the tallest trees,
ice-shagged, splintered,
holding up all of January

as if to give it back.
The highest branches rose
like the antlers of a startled elk.

There was no other way
but up, past the bent girders
over Cold Creek, through the small

fires of snow, layer after layer.
Winter's vault closed without a click.
Higher still where the road turned

into dirt and stone, tapering,
I got out to open the driveway gate
and felt my body grow tight

against the cold. There would be chores,
kindling to gather, a day's weather
in the satellite dish.

But for the time I stopped everything
to stand in the distance
of myself, turning white,

and could hear the thin ecstasy
of saws, the rise and fall,
a crackling in the hard wood.

❦

# ALL SAINTS EVE

Here where the last of October tears
at the tiny hinges of its great machine,
where all the ten thousand TV's stare
dazed as clear stones, lit with some bad dream
or other, some gang hit or dilapidated
condo, the fatal rubble of a ground floor,
we dress up our children like the dead,
though no one in particular, and scatter
them down the dark street. It's all a bit
too exciting, the shakiness of the dear
earth beneath them. You can see them skip
with pure white greed, expectant. It's nearly
criminal, this heaven—ah, to be young
and dead again. Go on, let your TV flicker
behind you. With every hungry bag they open,
a few sins fall in, the sweets they die for.

❧

# AIM

What child could resist the sweet sting
it fired into things, that ecstasy of glass,
how floodlights chipped and sputtered
when we cracked them, blackening over the dead street.

This was the future, a deeper euphoria
than cigarettes or money, however slight
our chances with such a minor rifle
and any but the most breakable of lives.

Our incompetence was mercy, the way it spared us
our little cruelties. And overhead
the question of our highest misses, if
they turned dangerous under the stars, falling.

How a gun loves a living target—any boy
will tell you—so I picked a sparrow,
a measly bird, yet when magnified
you could see it perched on a power wire,

the tiny black blisters of its gaze,
a pulse barely perceptible in its throat.
A part of me thought I'd never hit it
and still doesn't. Just as I fix it

in memory's scope, one eye closed,
the other locked in its circle, the bird
slips safely from the rifle's cross.
If I rush with giddy horror to the shuddering

feathers, at the end they disappear.
And in that moment as I fall away
from the world, I am wedded to it
and want nothing more than to give life

back through some slash in its fabric,
to walk straight as a bullet into the dead,
becoming radiant, necessary,
safer in their body than my own.

♣

# VACCINE

One more child in a silent line
of children, she braces for the cure
and its box of needles, the chilled
vials laid out in trays, clear
as gin, to stun the national blood.

But what does she know of the hope
that strikes a body like a fever?
Only the boy in a horrible book,
his chest pelted with little fires,
and over his brow a patch of cloth

warm and wrinkled like a hand.
The way he stares, that white blush
of brief exposure, his gaze stung
slightly in the camera-flash,
it's as if the future had thrown him

back, deeper into his strange flesh.
You'll feel a prick, nothing more,
the doctor tells her, though soon enough
the ache blooms beneath its scar,
so sore it's work, this taking in

of foreign cells, the carefully
enfeebled, their lives eclipsed
like porchlight in a pall of wings.
So many tiny bodies clasped
and shivering in her bloodstream.

In each a quiet misery,
she thinks, as if to reopen
a wound to see by, some dry
blister where it dots her skin,
pale and hardening like a star.

# MEDALS

By the mute parade of purple hearts
over my cousin's washroom wall,
I enter the dwarf pageantry
of the place: how little
I know, captive there.

I've seen others: Nazi medallions,
coins dipped in what I thought
was my blood, not having seen much
of blood or Nazis, the Asian cigarettes
cyphered into my cousin's arm.

When his body hung like a medal,
his chute pinned to the tallest branches,
proud boys held him in their crosshairs.
They never could make him talk.
Mostly he's quiet now.

To the others in their cells, he tapped
stories on a pipe with a spoon:
entire novels, Hollywood scripts.
Memory lengthened its holdings
the way wall-mirrors push their rooms clear into the yard.

He kept a schedule,
marked time by the bars of light
as they travelled over the floor.
If a day is a house,
sanity is a walk from room to room.

I hear the laughter of other rooms.
He has left something burning
sweetly in a dish.
I rinse my hands in its light,
unlatch the narrow door.

# REPORTS

### 1. Acoustic Shadows

*From only a few miles away, a battle sometimes made
no sound, despite the flash and smoke of cannon and the
fact that more distant observers could hear it clearly.*

As Lee pushed North and the dead flew
out of the fields in thick flocks
over Pennsylvania, the first, strange reports
went up over the wire:

from the medical tents on Wilson's Hill,
people could see the cannons
driving their nails of light
into the boarded house of the Union

and hear none of it. Who would have
believed things would go this far,
this long, the indestructible world
their intimate stranger?

For the Union soldier bound up
in what he saw, high in the near
silence, history was out there
beating its wings against the glass.

He would not move for the sight of it
and cupped his bowl of boiled coffee, watching.
All night men returned through the wild orchard,
their hands trembling like paper.

The wounded lay out on blankets in rows,
sleepless under the clear sky,
and the nails of remembered light
pinned them to their bodies.

## 2. Photograph of the 5th Vermont at Camp Griffin, Virginia

They would shake off the blanket of their shapes,
the black blurs that are horses and flags.
They would make a sport of it. A lark.
This much is clear. The avant mare tosses
the smoking cloud of her head unaware
of the photographer's count, the shutter
as it snips its measured ribbon of light.

The closer we look, the stronger the illusion
pulling away, leading us over the Braille
of a day in June, late, each man poised
to advance on the thin board of his shadow.
Here and there the details of lives beckon
with a small white heat: rings, teeth,
the grains of sun clinging to their fingers.

They will remember themselves, cautious
under the spry branches of Virginia.
They will remember themselves. And farther out,
more horses, flags; the river draped
over the earth like a photographer's cloak.

### 3. Confederate Dead

Small comfort, to have survived your name
and body, given over to the false tints
of painted slides, though, as we are often
led to believe, a dead man could do worse,

as in one of those accidents of charity
when the images were sold cheap, for the glass
at the heart of their tragic sentiment,
thousands of photographic slides raised
into the roofs of greenhouses. Go there.

See for yourself. Impossible as it is
to make out the red translucent cloth
and fire, the fog of sleeves, to trace
the man where he stood among so many

past misfortune he must have seemed
a phantom to himself. You never know.
You too might look up some day at the sheer
sky through the center of his body.

It takes a forgetful mind to enter the past
completely, the way we eventually do,
in our dotage perhaps or still later.
Or like the invisible man shell-
shocked from all feeling in his arm.

This too is how to survive your life,
to draw blanks over an effulgence
of scallions, blood tomatoes, the thick green air,
to be made singular in a true sense.

Or if not to survive it, to consume it
the way fire consumes itself, concealing.
Denial is like that, however ceremonious
or slight. The past eats and is eaten,

though it sometimes helps to think of this
as mercy. And it is. It takes years
of sun to bleach a phantom arm or flag, to turn
the way a widow turns her grief to her child.

No telling who she looks through now.
It's a comfort to think the dead there,
though they were always closest as a hunger,
a sinking into warm glass, unshattered, clear.

## 4. Postcard from Cold Harbor

So kind of you to write, to send this autumn
battlefield from Virginia, remembering how
I'm taken by the place: these flames of grass,
that monument sunk in the living embers.
And a sky not heaven but its frightened mirror,
the one bright cloud locked and floating.

I keep thinking of them there, the men
who stitched their names and cities in their shirts,
too serene as they spread their sewing
by the fire, pulled each wet thread between
their lips and slipped it into the needle's eye.

They narrowed their vision to see it,
making themselves small, sharp: so in time
they might follow the path of their letters,
so they might be carried off still warm
and shouldered into granary carts,
divided each from each. Under the idle
flapping of the coroner's tent, their names
would float from the patches on their backs,
sent out for a sheet of rock to lie in.

There would be voices to pronounce them,
the more difficult sounds repeated as questions.
And for a while it would seem generous
to talk this way, as if the names were so
many cases to tend to, for a year
or two, a generation at very most.
It would seem a personal reply:
the quiet surrounding these words like parks.

## 5. Taps

As night fell and the end of the world
brushed Atlanta with its black wing

beating a path through the embers,
men on either hill lowered their work

and looked up, listening. Somewhere
a rebel trumpet played slow and clear:

straight tones rustling vaguely at the ends.

Trees filled out their thin shirts.
The newly dead bent down in long arcs

into the circled breath of the boy.
There pressed against his teeth,

the force of grace reddened his tongue,
his cheeks, sweetened on his lips.

For a time the world burned unattended.
The sky's door swung gently on its hinge.

Music rolled in the beds of stones, grass,
all things and the breath that held their fire.

❧

# HOMAGE TO SZYMON LAKS

The flint, the shoe, the sip of water,
the hard currency of last effects,
the necessity, the razor, the broken cigarette,
the object itself unadorned and mute,
the wick, the lens, and him—what was he

in light of these things, a stick man
in zebra clothes and butcher hat, his life
boiled down to a stone at the bottom?
He too found it oddly barbaric:
the little flame of joy in his violin.

Still he kept it going, for want of other flames.
He was nothing indispensable,
as things are, though blessed, fit
to swell a mood or party, to animate a march.
Work, said the music, will make you free.

And how could he blame them, the ones
who cursed him, there, the kapellmeister
of Auschwitz, him and the whole makeshift
of bad instruments and uncertain hands:
the rosin, the spit valve, the splintered reed.

No telling when the next shower of blows
would fall or why, if there were reasons
to drive them or if they fell merely
for the pleasure: art for art's sake.
Birds weaved over the crematorium.

From a distance they were a flock of needles
closing a rip in the sky's cloth.
And always the unearthly legacy below:
the lamp, the chimney, the illumined tattoo;
the pillow stuffed with human hair.

Each day without warning another soloist
lost, tearing out a hole in sound.
And he rushed like water to fill it.
That, after all, is what the living do.
Mornings when the sky was cloudless and bitter

he wanted to believe the music would save him,
and it did, though not without a measure
of luck and guilt and the fear that sent
some men to the wires, demoralized by hope.
Or so he said. The shame of living

is never to outlive it. There were days
in winter it took everything he had
to move his stiffened hands, to curl inward
over his violin, shivering, his white breath
rustling on his fingers like a flag.

♣

# III.

# THE POSSIBLE

Once they were all we knew in the world,
the shapes of prayers and questions rising;
in radiant cribs, they curved up at the ends
of our voices. There was much to believe.
By a potted palm in the broken sun,

we felt them on our tongues like milk.
They slipped out of the names we gave them.
Once they rose in the wells of our bodies,
sprouted as hairs where the soil was darkest.
It was all we could do to keep them down.

Nights they backed away into the future
gazing at the body of the past, spread
themselves like a bride before a mirror.
We stood up too charmed to sleep and listened.
They made light of threats, promises.

When we cut them in two, each half-shuddered
in a fierce dream, they gave praise to no end.
How we wanted it to go on that way,
the evenings we stripped like oranges,
the soft, declarative fist of the heart.

But already we owed our lives to days
that refuse to straighten but come back
drifting in their arc, broken by horizons,
bearing down where we bend to drink, mourn,
brace ourselves for the world's return.

♣

# DOCUMENTARY

I watch your hospital TV as you sleep,
two weeks you sleep while men walk
in a silent movie, their world broken

into grains of documentary light:
a Cleveland street in the thirties, lanes
of laundry waving like women in a parade.

I have not watched long or close enough
to know why these men have come this far,
there on the verge of speech. Something

momentous is furling their white shirts.
The younger one talks fast with his hands,
his hair standing briefly in the wind;

the sky above them is raining the scars
of countless screenings. It may as well
be the future with its quiet insistence.

The way the asphalt blanches in fits,
it's as if the very ground below
were some grey scrim, a cloud swallowing

its radiant bolt. Elsewhere in Cleveland,
others are going about their lives.
From a closer time you would see the threads

of coalsmoke rising, hear the unconscious
clash of radios, a coathanger's chime,
the wasp sizzling in a bowl of cream.

A few will pause without reason,
towelling the warm platter, and recall
a cloudless afternoon when a father

or son said something that changed them,
*for good,* we say, thinking how it might
cross a mind four, five times maybe.

Take the moment we're living in: this vine
of serum, the bright hair floating in a fan.
Or the body sunk in the casement

of your body, the way it lies there
face-up in long, stationary walks.
Take the boy silently delivered

in a home movie, the one his parents watch
in silence. How quickly he forgets:
his face flushed, bursting like a match.

❧

# ELEGIAC STANZAS

Its heart giving out
off Kodiak Island, the white shadow
of itself a faithless portrait

greying into the Pacific drift.
There will be no story, no coming back.
The blowhole will yield its great,

drunken balloon, and no one will tell
what it is that sinks into green-
black clouds, seahorse and minnow,

the scores of tiny knives
scattering. If they flash away
in unison, bright fragments

of a single panic, there will be no center
to their fear. No shame
for the body, hardly a body

as it glides three months and more, to slip
into the Aleutian Trench,
dragging through the dull flare

of silt along the ocean floor,
its belly shark-torn, exposed,
the lazy door of its flank, swinging.

As its head gives under the sea-weight,
a cold brine rushing into the globe,
no plume of fluid will bear up

the burden of its proof.
Its darkness will be pure as heaven.
Natural causes, we would say

and do not. Either way, it is the consoling
that never explains,
how the bereaved move

in enquiring drifts
and back, shored over
the lip of some wave or other.

♣

# OPEN THROAT

In a child's game called dead man's float,
the winners are the most dead. It worries me
to my son's delight: how he spreads his lungs
like wings and glides over the deep end.
A web of light shadows the blue basin.

Say a soul rises when you dream it does,
and you wind up here in fear so pure
it turns into pleasure. Just like a boy
to take the worst into his waxen arms
as if it were fire. No use calling him now.

He is lost to himself, water-deaf, blind.
The charm is leaving the rope of his body.
You can see him fold into his blurred feet
then jump back through the sky's bright glass:
a child crowning into the world.

What luck! Or so we like to believe
however silly or fated it seems
later when the soft and vital parts
settle down into their dark work.
We could spend lives extending the lines

of our breath, close call after call,
delivered into one flushed affection
or another, the way a bad dream breaks
into the room it's in. We could spite
the literal heart into leaping

like a fish. My son gasps, refreshed.
It's how we come to defy gravity,
to holler backward through the open throat
at what it is that sleeps there, our bodies
pounding for admittance, swallowing air.

# GOLDEN DRAGON

The fish by the fortune cookies
at the Golden Dragon are little
more than the water they're in,
wrapped in the whorish light
of their body's chemise,

a sequinned debris of scarves
and paper fans. They are old.
Their sight is bad. Their feces
clear. Toothless, asthmatic,
they shimmy toward anybody's finger,

move their lips to read.
They live by the chance black rain.
The slightest sign and they rise
like prayers. We cannot know
the size of their happiness,

the gallons they need to forget
their way. The frail jaws crack
in our hands, and our slips
of fortune swim between us.
No one wheezes or loses their teeth.

The future wants us back again.
It knows how quick we are to hunger.
I lean through its paper door,
my body like a promise, feed myself
to the sweet remains.

# EASTER SUNDAY

The bell choir hurls its hymn of stones;
one late cue and everything stumbles
into heaven: He is Risen,
and they sit. It is all we can do
to contain ourselves, our cruel relief.

Children move down the doting aisle,
greedy for eggs. The pastor opens
to the flushed page in a large-lettered book.
He knows they are a tough crowd.
They would writhe out of their skin

into summer. Even the white scattering
of widows will not be still:
they shrink into their bodies,
smiling; all children look like theirs.
A fanfare stirs the lake of hymnals:

everyone stands, and the great
slur of praise shakes and rises.
The pastor reddens as he sings, wild,
famished, biting into the word *God.*
And then the pouring of the wine.

♣

# *ISAAC*

There are mountains, ask any believer,
where to wake suddenly is to risk
your life, where the spirit cold and fevered
would burn like rope in the body's fist,
so when I woke under the winter sky
last night, startled by the copper bell
of a goat above me, the way its eye
met mine I took it for a man or angel
or some such frightened thing. Like me it
darted backwards, tightening the thread
of sight between us. And so I slipped
a little farther out of sleep, my head
aching, my father mumbling where he lay,
one wakeful star above us like a blade.

♣

# FEAST OF THE SEVEN SORROWS

In the spectacle of heat near Corpus Christi,
where the cotton withers into bloom,
flashing its dry white fists, we curtain off
our southern bedrooms from the broad day
as if in illness or foreclosure.

Too hot to touch or bicker, we roll away
from one another and will not sleep.
Everything collapses like bad rage
or abandoned cars, and grief is what it is.
It clarifies on our tongues like salt.

Soon waiting becomes a religion of sorts,
and I look to the Feast of the Seven Sorrows
as a kind of union, summer to winter.
When the rain comes, we take it for a fire,
a blaze of needles over the wet street.

It trickles down the throats of gutters,
along the walls of rooms we wake to, hushed,
congealing into our flesh like snails.
They too go out to meet it, fire to fire,
trailing their bright secretions.

They climb our windows, their heads weaving
like blind musicians, and the world burns
down to its blue glass. We rise to it,
the way a wound rises into pain and higher
into talk and the memory of pain,

the way water rises in our gardens and tongues,
how we eye the steamed breasts of birds.
We open them with knives and blessings rising
to occasions. We pity them, the bodiless
wings. We take them to our lips and moan.

# LEGACY

The record needle lays down its thread
   of ruin, and the pianist dips
his hands into the crackling
   of small fires. They are old:
      this record, these hands.

If you listen close, you can hear
   the pianist humming as he plays,
      especially over the slurred passages,
unable to resist: his reserve
   stepping into the body
      of sound. He walks cautiously
through the minor movement,
   its slow recovery. His hands lift
      quiet as the ribs of a sleeping man.

All the hard hours come to this:
   a partial rest between query
      and lament, the way he commits
his flesh to memory, slips
   in the shapes of other hands.
      They descend; he descends.
They move apart, and he pauses
   on the steps to feel their pulse
      move out from his skin and wait there.

In my dream about Beethoven,
   he does not appear: my father
      keeps time to himself
slouching over the silent keys,
   his fingers curved as if listening
      were a kind of bodily capture.
In my dream about Beethoven,
   my father is driving his sons
      faster into the black woods of D-flat.
I wake startled. On every side,
   the great branches, falling.

After my father lost his memory
and will to play, he would sit
    in rooms listening to the scarred
        clarity of intimate pieces
or those like Beethoven's Ninth
    so loud it buried its hiss in joy's
        revolt. As words and faces
drifted from their moorings, the music
    remained the very water beneath him.


On the other side of what he heard,
I kept thinking of the man
    who watched his music pour
        soundlessly from the soprano's lips,
and went out to meet it, leaning
    through his past to hear.
        One voice wove through the others,
pulling its thread upward against the fabric.


The art of counterpoint,
    the man thought, is to raise independence
to the level of response.
    The way skin responds to skin,
        word to word.
Dissonance cadenced to its root,
    and for a moment the still world
        was the mirror of his own.


It haunts me: how he waited
    with his back to the applause,
        hearing nothing of the instant
where art ends,
    life begins.
        I like to think it moved him
to turn and see the shapes of joy
    step out of his silent body.

When my father died, he plowed a silence
through the homes of his sons.
    Some nights I am fitted with his
        cold hands and stare dumbly
at the keys. Impossible, these hands.
    They are what we blow into
        like dice, withdraw from the startled
backs of lovers. Take these

    as they fall onto separate pillows
        into thoughts that begin
with Beethoven and skim out over the face
    of the music. As the black current slides
        beneath them, what they see
is a traveling scar on the surface.
    They do not hear where the record ends,
        how the needle glides into the deaf wood,
the closing of the groove.

♣

# IV.

# NEW YORK MOVIE, 1939

*Homage to Edward Hopper*

Under an hourglass of lamplight,
the dim stair shuttles a tireless nothing.
It could be noon for all we know.

The usherette leans, silent, alone,
a deep blue shadow buttoned high
around her pale throat. The ribbon

on her pant leg shines thin as a fuse.
All around her the late are slipping out
of their coats, hushed and believing,

in each eye the glint and the fattening
reel that drives their own black tape.
Here in the dark they grow defenseless.

The projector beam burns back the layers
of its plot, and they part their lips to watch.
But for her it is the same gray strip

along the optic nerve: a few words broken
in lust and anger, the blurred roulette,
a tumbling car. She stares at carpets,

clicks the flashlight in her hand.
But then what did she expect? Nothing.
Which is to say, too much too well: all

in a day's work, she thinks, this idling
on the fringe of worlds too familiar
or strange to respond: this dark,

this room, this great stone column
the color of smoke. Her red rim
of flashlight brushes a man's sleeve.

Then it begins: though just what it is
she cannot say or prefers not to,
not even to herself. It simply comes,

the way squares of sunlight well up
on the side of a house, a corner office,
a quiet meal; or the way a bare white room opens out

onto the sea, how its merely being there
takes a certain freedom of movement.
It's as though solitude were the clear glass

of a painting we love, a cold drink
standing by a window in New England.
It is the lighthouse abandoned to the day,

what frees us to sink obsessed, the way sun sinks
into the eyelids of women on porticos,
what it presses into the warm stone.

Or there, in the red shadow splashed over
the foyer like a gown, the shush of waves
and usherettes so close we too are all

flashlight and stealth. Our very silence
tapers off into something less, more alive,
to part the fiery stillness of her curtain.

♣

# DIVORCE

It seemed so unlikely, how the wind shattered
into little sticks and pieces, the green
lengths of limbs coming off at the shoulder,
and rooftops sizzling under sparks of rain.

Then the power as it died in our freezers
wet with meat; and the startling of clocks,
how they opened the black dials of their eyes,
listening: somewhere a tiny motor clicked

on in the family pet, quiet as glass
the way it trembled, and what we breathed
darted back into our bodies and gasped.
It made us feel so meager, so small-boned

and curious; even as the weather raised
our cube of rooms to its ear and rattled,
we never woke completely, but always.
And though the storm dragged over us the world

grew strangely intimate, as if the more
it pried open with its hands, the farther
we would go and deeper, to feel it tear
our lives apart, skin from sleep, light from thunder.

❧

# BORN BLIND

A blind boy lies on a bright white table,
his eyes pried open as if gazing out
of his sleep at the surgeon's hand,
the slender blade and ascending tweezer.
He has never known the fear of darkness
or shiny objects, though when time comes
he imagines light stings a little. And it does.

When the nurse snips the gauze from his eyes,
he sees at last the terrible radiance
of her carved ring and silver scissor,
a map of blood vessels exploding on the wall.
How excited the room is and huge,
its lamp beaming with the emergency
of being there, each thing in a cry of color,

obsessively born into the world.
She holds a mirror to his face, and he traces
with his fingers the cold flat metal
of his breath, its bloom of erasure.
That night in bed, alone in the purity
of the unlit air, he realizes at once
the unspeakable poverty of it.

He closes his eyes, strikes a match
in his sleep, and a thousand shadows
dart away into the frightened
seams of things. That's what seeing is,
he thinks, not an end to blindness
but its continuous submission,
a thousand curious shards glinting.

♣

# RADIOGRAPHY

Nights like this my body would open
the iron door of a deeper rest.
Snow falls in a shower of pins.

It lights up out of nowhere
in the glowing radius of our house.
And all around me, the little clicks

of appliances and hot pipe,
this year's hatch of winter fleas,
the way our room contracts into

the cold hours, the way it swells.
My sleep has never been so sheer.
My husband slips into bed late

and mumbles, pulls the sheet to his lips
with a moan that is part comfort,
part complaint. I think of him

as two people longing to converge.
He cannot resolve the shapes
of questions, disagreements, whatever

leans into the half that listens.
Tempting, to take our wakefulness
with us, to lie facedown

in our wild hair, hands buried,
fingers curved like a watch-
maker god at a small creation.

Not that I am any less
the stranger to my husband's work,
his solitude, but I can't stop seeing

that room, those books, his photos
of the failing lamps in bodies.
There are days they could be anyone's:

this feathery shade of veins,
the pale oval lake of the bladder.
There in its glass, a glint of scars.

Last night by the subway window,
I watched my tired reflection
give way to the emergent light

of Oak Street Station and briefly revived.
As a native I tend to keep
my distance, but there on the live steps

I listened to the tenor player
bite into his reed and solo,
wincing over the high reaches and god

if I didn't envy the body
inside his body. He comes down
most days with an Orphean resolve,

his face afire in its skullcap,
especially deep into the ends
of phrases. It's as though the harder

he locks into the bright apple
of his sound, the more his breath
leads him, even as he shapes it,

raising up what his hands remember,
his black case gleaming with quarters,
eyes closed. Perfect health, my husband

once said, is a picture of night,
clear and starless, without fate.
What then does a body tell

anyone of the life it leads
into pleasure? Only a nonsense
of aches and wishes, a falling off

into memory and other bodies,
a shade younger perhaps, more faint,
wrapped in the sheer fabric

of our looking. I never told
my husband how it is sometimes,
how old encounters reemerge less

as a past than the unresolved
shapes of promise after promise.
I never told my husband all

the palmist said of what she saw there
and who, or what she thought I wanted
in her care to leave things open.

In her young hands, my heartline
lay under the stitch of tracks
tunneling into the white ore.

It's something I do for myself,
my husband being further from such things,
skeptical. I like to believe

we agree unscathed in our slight
withholdings, not to mention
the desires we keep from ourselves.

Though they rise beneath my knowing,
trailing in the intricate music,
the idea of them precedes me.

Say you wake up some night stunned
in refrigerator light,
staring into the vestibule,

and realize how little thought
it took to carry you there:
already you grow too large to return.

When the door closes, your shadow
becomes the room you're in.
You walk back to bed, a chill

of milk clinging to your lips.
In my best dream, I am no less
blind: I close my eyes to kiss,

listen, to go forward in my sleep.
Or like Beethoven in his death mask,
to sink into a deep sensation.

I've seen my husband like that:
contemplating a word he's lost,
still groggy under the booth

of rain our bay windows make.
There's scarcely a nerve below
he would not turn down like sheets.

In my favorite *Twilight Zone,*
what I love most is the moment
of discovery, when the boy who gets

his one wish for x-ray vision,
so thrilled to see his girlfriend
whole, burns a channel of sight

past the brief arrival of skin
to the weird labor of her
physical heart. He gazes clear

into its chambers, though only
for a moment there, and through,
where suddenly we find ourselves

at the morning end of a mere dream.
We're a kind of radium that way,
outwardly serene, the bits of us

sparking under our eyelids.
It's how I picture the inventors
of heaven, the way they bow their heads

in a heightening of senses.
They are leaning over something
glittering in the dark, some plate

of water with the sky in it.
Never so clear as in that silence
before a big meal in winter;

just inches from their grateful teeth,
the cooked meat perspiring.
Who can condemn them for the world

they've made, the beautiful machines
of cathedral organs, that wine-
red glass and wax smoke? It sweetens

their bread to think of it: the idea
of a buried, more brilliant life.
They take it on their tongues,

douse the little flames there,
and mumble sleeplessly. To take
and be taken. Not to reject

the world, but to finish it
in their minds, to give it an end
as if it too were a body,

beautiful once and driven,
to hold it the way one body
holds another, how we hold our own,

looking down in bathroom showers
at the slow fuse of being alive.
These nights I lie still as glass

and feel my very cells divide,
alert to sleep or a husband's touch.
Mostly I drift off just this side

of dawn. The snow, if it snows,
turns clear in the black dirt.
Each cold seed is opening.

♣

# ACKNOWLEDGMENTS

Poems in this book first appeared in the following journals:

*Agni:* "Medals" (appeared as "Medals: a Processional of Rooms");

*Chelsea:* "Born Blind";

*Denver Quarterly:* "Aim";

*The Georgia Review:* "Homage to Szymon Laks";

*Hawai'i Review:* "Golden Dragon";

*The Journal:* "Postcard of Atomic Bomb Test, Yucca Flat, 1953";

*The Laurel Review:* "All Saints Eve";

*The Missouri Review:* "Legacy," "Book of the Living," "Acoustic Shadows";

*The Paris Review:* "Naked Eye," "Documentary," "Pomegranate";

*Poetry:* "Taps," "Host";

*The Quarterly:* "Easter Sunday";

*Quarterly West:* "New York Movie, 1939";

*Queen's Quarterly:* "North: 1991";

*Sewanee Review:* "Confederate Dead," "Photograph of the 5th Vermont at Camp Griffin, Virginia," "Postcard from Cold Harbor";

*Shenandoah:* "Cardinal," "The Possible";

*The Southern Review:* "Caravaggio: The Supper at Emmaus," "Elegiac Stanzas";

*The Threepenny Review:* "Open Throat," "Divorce";

*Western Humanities Review:* "Radiography," "Feast of the Seven Sorrows," "Isaac";

*The Yale Review:* "Native Tongue".

"Homage to Szymon Laks" appeared in *Best Texas Writing 1996.* "Caravaggio: The Supper at Emmaus" received the Milton Dorfman Poetry Award. "Cardinal," "The Possible," "Taps," "Caravaggio: The Supper at Emmaus,"

"Elegiac Stanzas," "North: 1991," and "Legacy" were selected for the *Quarterly Review of Literature Poetry Series: 50th Anniversary Anthology.* "Pomegranate" received a Billee Murray Denny Prize and appeared in the anthology *The Denny Poems.* Also, several poems appeared in two chapbooks entitled *Broken Circle* (Ring of Fire Award, Archangel Books) and *The Possible* (Gerald Cable Award, Silverfish Review Press). Special thanks to the Corporation of Yaddo and the MacDowell Colony for their kind support.

Thanks as well to Scott Cairns, Nicki Cohen (mon amour), Jeffrey Donaldson, Albert Goldbarth, Jeanine Hathaway, Anthony Hecht, Donald Justice, Julia Kasdorf, Laura Kasischke, Ross Leckie, Marjotie Maddox, Richard Spilman, and the folks at BOA—Bob Blake, Steve Huff, Thom Ward, and Al Poulin (the late great)—for their help during the completion of this book.

And finally, the deepest gratitude goes out to so many teachers, especially Burton Feldman, Bin Ramke, Donald Revell, and Robert Pinsky for their generosity and inspiration at a pivotal time in the author's life.

Epigraph, page 9, from *"La Venue a l'écriture"* originally published in *La Venue A l'écriture* by Hélène Cixous, Madeline Gagnon, and Annie Leclerc (Paris: Union Generale d'Editions, 10/18, 1977). Collected in *Entre L'Ecriture* (Paris: Des Femmes, 1986) Copyright © 1986 by Editions des Femmes. The version that appears here was translated by Deborah Jensen, with modifications by Ann Liddle and Susan Sellers, and appearing in *Coming to Writing and Other Essays,* edited by Deborah Jensen, Copyright © 1991 by the President and Fellows of Harvard College. Reprinted by permission of Harvard University Press.

♣

# ABOUT THE AUTHOR

After earning a Master of Arts degree in Music Performance from the Lamont School of Music and working for several years as a classical and jazz guitarist, Bruce Bond went on to receive his Ph.D. in English from the University of Denver. His previous books of poetry include two full-length collections, *Independence Days* (Robert Gross Award, Woodley Press) and *The Anteroom of Paradise* (Colladay Award, *Quarterly Review of Literature*), and four chapbooks. He has received fellowships from the Bread Loaf Writers' Conference, the Sewanee Writers' Conference, the Wesleyan Writers' Conference, Yaddo, the MacDowell Colony, and the Virginia Center for the Creative Arts. He is Director of Creative Writing at the University of North Texas and poetry editor for the *American Literary Review*, and continues to perform classical music and jazz in the Dallas-Fort Worth area.

# BOA EDITIONS, LTD.

## AMERICAN POETS CONTINUUM SERIES